Struggle Trauma Nor Bad Choices Stopped Me

From Trauma to Triumph

Felicia M. Streeter

Struggle, Trauma, nor Bad Choices Stopped Me, is dedicated to girls/women all around the world who feel hopeless because of past choices & mistakes. This book will inspire you and help you to realize that there is still a happy, fulfilling, & bright future waiting for you if you let go of your past, live in the present, and be hopeful about your future. Ladies know that it's ok to make mistakes that we learn from, it is the ones that we don't learn from that causes the most regrets!!!

TAKE BACK YOUR POWER LADIES~YOU ARE IN CONTROL.

Dedicated to my sister: Tracy L. Streeter

God-daughter: Tanika Hebron

Nieces: Ronda & Iyanna Streeter & Melinda Russell

Great Nieces: Alize & Alexis Streeter

& My Mentees

Special thanks to: Dana Mitchell for sharing her story

Author: Debra Clifton-Mitchell (No relation to Dana) for her guidance & advice during this book journey

Dr. Catherine Eason-Editor & Mentor.

To My Kids: Taronn Davis & Jermaine Blackmon

My Grandkids: Taron Davis Jr. & Zarriah Hardy

Everything I accomplish is an attempt to make you both proud of me. I love you both more than words can explain, which I show through actions, discipline & teachings.

To God be the Glory!

CONTENTS

Introduction

As children, we all have plans, aspirations, and dreams. Most times, with guidance, support, and ambition they come true. Unfortunately, things do not always go as planned. My plans were to be in my career field by age 25, which was family counseling. I planned to be married by age 30, have two kids, one boy, one girl, and retired by age 50. After retirement, I would do only what I was passionate about, which is being an advocate for people who needs assistance in life, especially women & their children. Well, here is what really happened....

JOURNEY 1

The Adams Family

I do not remember a lot about my childhood, but most of my memories start from about age 11 when I met a lady named Mrs. Adams, who called herself my Godmother. I remember her first name as Sarah. The role she played in my life was very significant. I did not have a spiritual family, so I didn't know anything about God. I am sure my mom & dad believed in him, but it was never talked about in our household.

I met her through a childhood friend of mine who we called Yogi, which was her daughter. I am almost sure they called her that because she put you in the mind of yogi bear. (Yogi Bear was the first breakout character created by Hanna-Barbera and was eventually more popular than Huckleberry Hound)

At any rate, we lived in the same building on Central & Huron, in Chicago IL. Their house always seemed dark, clammy, and cold, which put me in mind of the TV show, "The Addams Family." Which aired from 1964-1966, then was converted into a movie and released in theaters in October 2019. A show about a weird, funny, fun-loving family who lived in a dark, clammy mansion.

I saw what it was to be unequally yoked, but of course at that age had no idea what it was. Her husband was the total opposite of her. He did not go to church; he drank, smoked cigarettes, and cursed a lot. He never expressed or had conversations to show that he believed in God. (No judgement) He was rude & mean. I remember asking my friend, "Why does your mom stay with him, he is so mean, they are so different?" She shrugged her shoulders.

I attended church with them every Sunday & Tuesday. It felt good going. I felt at peace whenever I attended. At first, I just enjoyed the dinner and desert that was served right after service then I started enjoying the choir. It was a pleasant sound that put my soul at ease. Although I couldn't sing, I later joined. After going for months and getting more into the word, I loved it! I wished that my family would go and hear of this great spiritual being. One Sunday, something amazing happened!

I was filled with what people said was the holy ghost. Something took over my body and I couldn't stop moving, uttering unfamiliar words, and crying tears of joy. After I was released from this thing that I didn't understand, my God-mother said, "You're special." The other kids said I was weird because they didn't understand what happened. I felt even closer to God after that day. (It was the God in me!) As of that day, I knew I was a child of God! I didn't understand what happened to me, so I never spoke of it again. What language was I speaking? What was the light I seen while I was filled with what is said to be the holy spirit? I don't know, but it was a great experience that I will never forget it.

When Mrs. Adams and her family moved, I was age 13 and had nobody to attend church with. I felt like I had separated from God. At age 18 I started visiting different churches on my own, until I found one that felt good to me. My mom and brothers barely attended, so I started taking my younger cousins. I did not want them to miss the opportunity to have a relationship with God. They enjoyed it. I continued my journey with God in it. I got re-baptized at age 20 because I understood the meaning of it more as an adult, than I did at age 12. Where would I be, had I not met this sweet, short lady, who called me her Godchild? I don't even want to imagine. I believe everything happens for a reason because I met her. I was introduced to a pheromenal spiritual being. Wherever this lady is, if she is still alive, I pray that God blesses her for introducing me to him. I am forever grateful!!!

If you have somebody who has made the slightest difference in your life, helped or supported you in any way, you should show them much love and gratitude. Nobody owes you anything, especially after you are an adult, so appreciate them.

JOURNEY 2

Bad Choice in a Man

❦

How did I not see the signs, or did I just ignore them? Yes, that's it, I ignored them. At age 15 I met the father of my oldest son. He was 17 at the time we met, which made him 2 years older and more advanced than I was. He was so sweet and protective of me, which I thought was cute until being protective turned into possession. When we first started dating, we use to take long walks in the park and talked about everything. He would go to the local Vienna restaurant to pick up food for us to eat. We never went to the movies, or ate at dine in restaurants, just the basics as teenagers without a car.

We dated for about 4 months, then he took me to his house to meet his mom. She was very nice and soft spoken the first time I met her, but as time went on, she became mean, as if to be jealous of our relationship. No, couldn't be I thought, since she was his mother, not his ex. Though it is said, That mothers can sometimes be unconsciously jealous that she is losing her son to a girlfriend/wife. While visiting, she told him that I could not come over on Mondays because cross-eyed people were bad luck on that day. (Fixed at age 32 with cosmetic surgery) He saw the look on my face, tears built up in my eyes, (I was very sensitive at the time) so he launched at her and grabbed her by the neck. She fell back on the couch and his sisters grabbed him off of her. What she said was very mean and hurtful, but not a reason for him to react that way with his own mom. I felt that a verbal-respectful checking would have been sufficed. **Warning #1**

I stayed home for a few weeks until things calmed down. He started coming to my house to hang out, my mom was nicer and more lenient, which is not always a good thing. After a year we became closer. I started being sexually active at age 16. He became more emotionally attached and more protective, or should I say possessive. One time we got a visit from an old friend who was my oldest brothers' friend. He came in, spoke to everyone, and gave us all hugs. I guess he was surprised to see how I had matured physically. I started to have curves, breast, and fill out. I was skinny when we were younger. He complimented me several times and made the statement; "The ugly duckling has turned into a swan." We all laughed, but my boyfriend Ty didn't laugh at all. He had this grim look on his face as he walked away. I assumed he went to the bathroom, but later found out he was waiting for Ed downstairs in the hallway. We heard yelling, then what seemed to be a loud smack, or cracking sound. We all ran downstairs and Ed was laid out on the hard marble floor with blood coming from his face. There was so much of it- that we couldn't tell where it was coming from. After rinsing his face while another person called the ambulance, we realized that his nose and mouth was bleeding profusely. Ty did it!

Warning #2

I stayed away from him for weeks after that incident, just to later give in after his begging and pleading for forgiveness. As time went on, I noticed more signs of indirect control, manipulation, and possessive behavior, but ignored it, because of what I thought was **love**. The reality of it is that I was afraid & weak.

Then came the signs of drug use. I had never been around drug use in that time of my life, but lots of alcohol abuse. I had no inclination that he was on drugs until I was hanging out with him in the basement of their home. I went to use the bathroom where his younger sister and one of her friends was. It didn't bother me to use the bathroom in front of them because we were all females and we were really cool. They had a plate on the sink with brown colored powder on it. The substance was moving around on the plate. His sister asked if I wanted to try it. I said, "No! It looks gross, what is it?" She said, "Its dope, you snort it, and it will make you feel better than you have ever felt in your life, go ahead and try it." A quick thought flashed through my mind, it won't hurt, they do it, and there is nothing wrong with them. I opened my mouth to say okay, but the word no came out. I felt relieved. She said "My brother-your boyfriend does it." The other girl said, "Don't force her, she couldn't handle it anyway, she still has milk behind her ears." I was offended because they were only a year older than I was. Oh well I thought, I didn't want to do that stupid crap anyway. I washed my hands and went back into the sitting area where he was still watching TV waiting on me to return. I looked upset so he asked, "What's wrong?" With a frown on my face and frustration in my voice, I asked; "Do you use drugs???" He looked confused, but angry. "Who told you that, he yelled?" I looked at the bathroom door, he called his sister from the bathroom and started to yell at her about the question I presented to him. She started laughing, stating that she was just joking. I felt relieved, but not convinced, just to find out later that it was true. I was heartbroken. I started to wean myself from the relationship.

He noticed that I was pulling back so he started to change his behavior. Well, of course it did not last long, because it's hard to change who you are after being that way for so long. Months later, while walking back to his house from the park, we encountered a young man repairing his car. He asked my boyfriend to give him a hand. Ty responded, "I'm with my lady, I can't help you." The guy asked again, saying "I won't take too much of your time." He responded with frustration, "Like I said, I can't help you!" The guy went on to say, "Well how about I make your lady help me then?" Ty went into a rage, almost like the Incredible Hulk. He picked the car jack up from the ground and hit the guy in the mouth with it. The guy fell to the ground, I'm standing there in shock as the man fell holding his face. Cold chills went through my body, my teeth felt piercing pain, as if I had gotten hit. We took off running to the house. He wasn't afraid at all. He had lots of uncles and brothers, but me on the other hand, I was scared to death, and it didn't help to find out later that the guy was a well-known gang banger (an unknown vice lord). Word on the street was that he was going to have us both killed.

Warning# 3

I stayed low for a while; I was an emotional wreck. I did not know much about street stuff, but I had seen enough movies to know, these types of people would actually kill you, then go out to eat dinner, and sleep like babies. It cooled down after a few months, because his uncle spoke with someone from the gang and got the incident squashed, as they say, which meant, we didn't have to worry about retaliation. Although he had never physically hurt me, he had hurt other people because of me. I felt bad, guilty, confused, afraid, so I started avoiding people to protect them. I wouldn't speak to men or give eye contact, in fear that he would hurt them, or that he would be killed in the process of his possessive behavior over me.

In the winter things were pretty calm, I avoided him as much as possible. Although I still had love for him, I didn't like him anymore. In the spring of that next year, my family and I moved. I wish it had been out of town to get away from him, but it was just 1 mile from both of our old addresses. I broke up with him several times, but the threats to commit suicide brought me right back.

There are several reasons why we make bad choices in men, or reasons why we stay after we realizes we made a bad choice:

- No teachings on healthy relationships.
- Rushing into relationships without getting to know the person.
- Afraid of leaving after we are in the relationship because of abuse.
- To live a certain lifestyle that the man provides.
- For protection.

- For love.
- Afraid of being lonely/alone.
- Convince ourselves that we cannot do any better.
- Do not want to start over, so we stay and waste more time.

When Love turns into abuse, control, physical or emotional pain, don't make excuses to stay, give yourself reasons to leave. Remember to love yourself more than you love a man, especially one who is not good to you, or for you.

When I discussed my book with one of my really good friends, she wanted to tell her story, which had me in tears and helped me understand why she made bad choices in men. Here's her story.

Dana Mitchell: I have never been around healthy relationships which is part of the reasons I made bad choices in men, along with other reasons. I was molested as a child and raped as a young adult. When you encounter such trauma, it can affect your way of thinking, the choices you make, and how you live your life. I felt worthless and not of value. All my childhood and young adult life, I wondered why nobody protected me, or why was I a target to be treated that way? At age 18, I was raped by a well-known pimp who later became an actor, whose name I cannot state according to the author. No, I was not one of his working girls. He was a friend of our family, which is why I felt safe getting in the car with him.

One night after leaving the Clique night club starring Adina Howard, he called me to the car and asked if I needed a ride home. To avoid waiting on a cab, I said "Yes." I would have never imagined that his plan was to rape me. I got in the car, put the seat belt on, and he said I looked sexy, and continued the conversation by asking how was the family? I responded that everybody was doing well. He proceeded to drive and said he needed to stop by his moms to give her medicine and make sure she was okay. I thought that was so sweet coming from a man. We arrived at this 2-flat building on the west side of Chicago, he asked me to come in because it would be rude to leave me in the car. I unfastened my seat belt and went into the apartment with him. He locked the door, pointed me to the couch, and walked to the back towards the kitchen speaking out loud as to be talking to his mother. He came back with rope and grabbed me by my arm, taking me into a bedroom. I instantly start crying and screaming hoping that his mom would come stop him, although at that point, I knew that the story about his mom wasn't true. He hit me and said shut up bitch, can't nobody hear you. He raped me repeatedly, then sat on the edge of the bed to take primo breaks. (Marijuana laced with cocaine)

I laid there angry at myself for getting in the car with him. I blamed myself for wearing sexy/provocative clothing. I was so scared! Why was there no one around to protect me? How could he do this to me? He knows my family. When he finally untied me, he threatened me, and said to never tell. I agreed, just to get out of there alive. He dropped me off to my aunt's house on Laramie & Augusta. I called my aunt while she was at work and told her I had been raped by him. She said to keep my mouth shut, that we would discuss it when she got home from work. I guess she never made it home, because the subject never came up again. I was hurt and confused. Did she think I was lying, was she protecting him instead of me? Why did she sweep this under the rug?

He would come up the block periodically, call me to the car to make sure I hadn't told anybody. He would give me gifts and money. I accepted hoping that he would leave me alone. This went on for almost a year, then not as much. I started dating a guy from the neighborhood who was hardcore and of the streets. One day my rapist came up the block while my new guy & I were outside on Laramie, he called me to the car. I looked up at Dee, as if to get the okay for me to go to his car. He asked, "Why is he calling you to his car? He is a well-known pimp." Tears built up in my eyes and fear ran through my body. I told him that we would discuss later, as we did, and he promised to protect me, which he did, and my rapist left me alone.

I later got the courage to report the rape to the police station in my district where I lived but the deadline to report rape statute of limitations had expired. I feel better after having the courage to attempt to report it, as well as vented to family and friends later about what I had been through, and how the rape affected my life. I can now begin to heal.

Just to later have the same man who protected me to mistreat me and throw the rape in my face. He forced me to have sex with his friends, when I said no, he would punish me by spraying my vagina with roach spray and beating me. Now who was going to protect me from him?

Ladies being controlled & abused is scary and can sometimes lead to death. I encourage you to get out early. It is your human right to choose happiness & safety over the love or fear of a man. You have the power, it is your choice to choose you. Take back your power from men who control, abuse, & manipulate women. Let supportive family members and friends know your plan to leave so that they can help you with a safe exit plan. Use all resources like police and support groups.

The human body is strong. but not intended to be a punching bag, or to endure physical abuse.

The hands of a strong, angry, enraged man, can kill you with his bare hands. Love is a beautiful thing, but surely not worth dying for.

Turn the emotion of fear into courage and fight back. Not with your fist, because a man is much stronger than a woman usually, but fight back with the will to live!!!

I understand that it is not easy to leave a man that you love, or even fear, but it is surely worth it. You are worth it!

Reflection: Bad Choice in a Man

_____

_____

_____

_____

_____

_____

_____

_____

_____

_____

_____

_____

_____

_____

_____

_____

_____

JOURNEY 3

Trauma

After so much emotional stress I miscarried without knowledge of being pregnant. At this time, I was 17 years old. This is what led up to this traumatic night. We sat on the hall steps of the two flat building where I lived. He begged me to take him back and to have sex with him. I said no, but he continued to beg and plead, saying; after this he would never ask again. But he missed me so much he didn't know what to do, that he couldn't eat or sleep. I was adamant, again, I said NO! Hoping that he would give up, but he didn't. Then the begging turned into threats, so here I am on the hallway stairs, praying that someone would come out and rescue me, it didn't happen. He pulled my underwear to one side, allowing him to thrust into my vagina. I was sick to my stomach, I closed my eyes and prayed that he would hurry, and he did, in less than 5 minutes, he was done. I went in to shower and never returned to where he was. He called my name several times, but I didn't respond. I cried myself to sleep, angry because he wouldn't just leave me alone, but sad because I felt bad for him.

That night I woke up out of my sleep due to some discomfort to my lower stomach. I got out of bed and went to the bathroom, as I pulled my pajamas down to sit on the toilet, blood clots soaked my underwear, and it looked like little chopped pieces of liver. The blood wouldn't stop no matter what I tried. I stood up from the toilet to wet a towel and blood was pouring out of my vagina. I had never seen anything like this before in my life. I thought I was having a bad dream. The small 36 square feet bathroom was filled with blood. I felt myself getting weak. After doing everything I could to stop the bleeding, I called out for help. My aunt came before my mom did.

I saw the shock/fear on her face. She started to grab dry towels from the linen closet, six dry towels were soaked in blood, and she called out for my mom to call the ambulance. I remember riding in the ambulance alone, I was as scared as I felt myself going in & out of consciousness. I remember thinking, is my life about to end at age 17. Although I knew my mom loved me, she wasn't supportive. I guess she couldn't be what she didn't know how to be. Her mom wasn't supportive to her. She didn't know how to give what she didn't receive. I arrived at a hospital on Division Street, named St. Anne's at the time, now it's named Bethel New Life. I had to get a blood transfusion, because according to the nurse, I had lost 4 pints of blood, which was half the blood in my body. She said "God loves you, he kept you, because it only takes five minutes to bleed to death. The average young adult body holds 8-9 pints of blood, you lost a little over 4 pints, so consider yourself special. She spent a lot of time with me because she knew I was afraid and had no support system. Later my mom arrived at the hospital, with a bag of clothes, because the pajamas I wore were drenched in blood and had been discarded. I didn't even call him. Sadly, I think I was relieved to have lost the baby, only to have his child 2 years later.

Yes, I went back to him after 5 months of us being broken up after the miscarriage. At this point I didn't love him anymore, but I figured he must love me to be this consistent, as if he really could not live without me. That thought didn't keep me for long though, because I learned that even consistency was a part of running game. I left him after I turned 18. I found out I was pregnant three months after the breakup, and no, I did not go back. Good for me, but bad for my child, who would be raised in society without a father. By the time my son turned 3 years old, his father was in and out of jail due to his drug addiction. What was even worse, I never returned to school after the traumatic miscarriage, but after years of procrastination, I returned to school and earned my G.E.D. and went on to college.

Ladies, when these men show you who they are, believe them. Don't waste years of your time hoping he gets better. Love should never hurt, or be emotionally stressful. We cannot change a man, but our nurturing spirit as women makes us believe that we can. A man, or any person has to believe they need to change before the process can begin. Some men believe they have a right to beat/control their girlfriends/women if she does not conform to their way of thinking, or their control tactics. Save yourself the regret of wasted time and emotional scars.

Reflection:

_____

_____

_____

_____

_____

_____

_____

_____

_____

_____

_____

_____

_____

_____

_____

_____

_____

JOURNEY 4

History Repeats Itself

I will not say that I had not learned anything, but when it came to settling and relationships, I had allowed it to be a repeated offense. After the relationship with my first son's father, I had a few relationships in between. They were okay relationships, some lessons, some blessings. I will not say they were a waste of time, because they helped me grow into the woman I have become. They did not last, or result in marriage, either because of being young and not ready for commitment, or not being a good fit.

Although I was young, I always looked for husband qualities in a man, especially after being introduced to church by my Godmother Mrs. Adams. I have no idea why I stuck around after I saw that those qualities were not evident. Was I dickmatized, or was it love that kept me around... I'm sure a little bit of both. This could be a good reason to have sex after marriage. You know what you are feeling is real and not sexual emotions.

I was not in a hurry to get married, but I knew it was something I looked forward to once I became a mature adult and with the right person. One thing I promised myself was to never be so in a rush to be married that I settled for anybody to be my husband. Making a bad choice in a husband can cause you to be miserable while married. I had seen and heard this a lot from married couples. Don't do it to yourself ladies. I always said that I would have a husband so that God could be proud of me. I tried to be the best person I could be and to treat my body as a temple because I felt like he (God) was watching me. I was always kind to people, I tried to keep a pure heart & mind. I felt like my only sin was sex without marriage; foolish mortal! So, I thought if I got married that I would be perfect in his eyes. Well, of course now that I am older, I know that I could never be perfect in his eyes, but I figured getting close to it was okay with me. I took a break from relationships, got re-baptized, then along came a spider, and sat beside her, and I got caught in the web. The cycle of making bad choices in men was repeated.

Here is how it all began. He was cool, funny, tall, dark, and had swag, so I ignored the fact that he was 21 with 4 kids, 3 baby mothers, living the street life with no job. He had lots of potential, but chose not to use it for good. He was fun and did not mind spending money. Money never excited me or got my attention and it did not this time either, but it was good to know that he was not cheap. He did not take care of me, but he made sure I was okay enough to stick around. I think the money was more like payment to ignore the cheating. He was one of those men who thought he could pay for you to shut up and take whatever he dished out. I wanted to see the good in people instead of seeing them for face value. I always gave the benefit of the doubt and never wanted to judge people according to past mistakes, as I had a few of my own.

One summer day, I was sitting on the porch looking as cute as could be, I was scintillating, with blonde streaks in my hair, pretty smooth caramel skin, and an hour glass shape, with an amazing personality. I heard a voice ask the girl on the porch next to me, "Who is that?" The female voice said, "Ask her yourself." I turned around to give him my name and seven years later a baby boy was born.

The first 2 years were pretty smooth while getting to know each other, besides a little drama here and there. We had lots of fun dating, meeting his friends & family made me feel special. He took me to places & restaurants that I had never seen or heard of. As time went on, he stopped hustling and got a job working with K-9 security. Had I known that he loved dogs because he was one, I probably would not have stuck around for so long. I think the saying is true, good girls like bad boys, and opposites attract, or maybe that is just some crap women made up as an excuse. We later moved in together. (Bad idea) That is when I noticed the cheating signs. When I spoke up about things I discovered, that is when the verbal & physical abuse started. My oldest son disliked him because he mistreated me and he felt the tension & negative energy. Do you know that psychology research studies show that your kids lose respect for you when they see that you don't stand up for yourself? Yes, this is true. I learned this in early childhood 102. I regret subjecting my son to that. (I asked him to forgive me when I learned the effects it has on kids)

He was very controlling, which I later found out was a part of his history with women. The physical abuse didn't last too long after it started, because I was not going for it, but should not have put up with it for as long as I did. The cheating & emotional abuse continued though. He once told me that I had a smart mouth and was uncontrollable. After realizing that he did not have my best interest, I didn't want to be with him anymore, nevertheless be his wife. After a long 12 years (1998-2010) of some wasted time, mixed with some good experiences, but mostly bad ones, one miscarriage, one abortion, one black eye, one busted lip with stitches, fractured nose, one bruised heart, many hurt feelings, and making excuses to accept cheating because I had no proof, although intuition made it clear, I was finally done. I remember thinking of stabbing him with my ice pick like Chucky did victims in his movies, but could not even fathom hurting someone that I loved. Thinking to myself, why was it so easy for him to hurt me? Ladies the answer is; most people do not know how to love, so a lot of times your definition and theirs will not be the same.

Their insecure and hurting inside themselves, for reasons that they will never share because of embarrassment or ego, so they inflict the pain they feel on others. I also learned that love also means letting go. Letting go is always better than inflicting pain back and forth as pay back in relationships. It is not wise to pay back pain with pain, just leave! The girls he cheated with would never tell on him & he never got caught red handed. I knew he was immature and a cheater, but because we were young, I really didn't expect much more. I was foolish enough to think as long as I came first and they were willing to be his little secret(s) that they were the ones stupid, not me. I later realized we all had low self-esteem and apparently didn't know our self-worth to be willing to put up with that type of treatment. After deep thought I realized I had stayed with him so long because of our son. I was one of those girls, like many, who hoped to live a fairytale life as a family with the father of their child. That should not be seen as a fairytale though. It should be our reality. We should have husbands and families and not baby daddies with broken homes left to parent on our own.

My worst memory of him was:

When a romantic night at the hotel turned into fright night. He got jealous when a young man said that I was sexy while we were out getting dinner. I replied saying "Thanks for the compliment." When we returned to the room he asked where I knew the guy from. I responded by saying; "I don't." I proceeded to go take a shower. After I returned to the sitting area in this beautiful spacious room at the Champaign Lodge, he grabbed me by my neck and slammed me to the floor. I was shocked, I got up and grabbed the phone in an attempt to call the police. He snatched the phone out the wall and wrapped the cord around my neck. The room started spinning and getting dark. I took the phone receiver part of the phone and hit him in the face with it, when he released me I ran out the door forgetting that I was naked and fresh out the shower. He ran behind me, caught up to me, and covered me by wrapping his arms around me, pulling me back into the room. I went freely after realizing I was naked. He said he was sorry-I forgave him. In my simple mind, it was my fault for making him jealous.

Well, I have learned to live by K-Michelle's song, You can't Raise a Man, verses allowing Mary J's song to become my national anthem, I Love My Mr. Wrong. Ladies no matter what you have heard or seen growing up, there are good men out here, and chivalry still exist. There are mature men in the world who was raised with morals, dignity, and they have the upmost love & respect for women. Rushing into relationships, or being in unhealthy ones is only a distraction, and most times only hold you back from the good things and men who are waiting for you.

The misconception of love: Based on faulty thinking we assume we should tolerate mistreatment because we love a person, or because they claim to love us. We listen to songs that talk about love hurts and assume it's normal. We most times see our moms, cousins, role models, and others around us endure pain in relationships, so we think it is okay. Love should not hurt intentionally. If two people come to an agreement that we love each other, but not meant for each other, so it's best to depart, then that's okay. That is a mature decision that may hurt, but it is a hurt that you can heal from without scars. There were no games played, or stringing along. This type of breakup is worth a little bit of pain, but lies, cheating, deception, false promises are not good. So, unbrainwash yourselves and know that love should feel good-not hurt.

I took a break from relationships after 2010 for self-care: The practice of taking an active role in protecting one's own well-being & happiness. I realized that being in a relationship is not mandatory, although they feel good when it's with the right person. I cut my feelings off completely when I turned forty. I was fed up!!! I felt absolutely nothing for him. I realized my time was too precious to go backwards and if it didn't work the first time, 9 out of 10 times it won't work the second or third time. I have not entered into another toxic relationship after him. I vowed to make better choices!!!

I started thinking of what type of woman I was and my potential, so I asked myself, "Why do you settle for such a man?" Because he is the father of my child.... So! Because you all have history together.... So! Because you don't want to start over... So! Because I was afraid that no other man would want a woman in her forties, with two kids, by two different fathers... So! Because he had ruined my self-esteem by saying repeatedly that I was not as cute and vibrant as I was in my twenties... So! That didn't change the fact that I was still beautiful inside and out. Words hurt and stick with us, but we have the power to rebuild what men tore down and remember what self-esteem means: Confidence in one's self, how you think and feel about you, not how someone else perceives you.

When you look in the mirror and someone beautiful is looking back at you, but after being told so many times that you're ugly, you're old, you're not what's happening anymore, you're not short/tall enough, you don't have certain talents, you start to believe it. Ladies you are everything you believe you are, so stop giving someone else the power to dictate who you are. From one woman to another, you are beautiful.

Stop saying "I tolerate him because I love him and start saying I won't tolerate any man because I love myself!" We can no longer allow love to make choices for us, we have to make choices for love. Everybody we love are not meant for us to be with.

Self-esteem: confidence in one's own worth, or abilities; self-respect; self-confidence.

The key word in all these words are; **Self** We should not give a man that much power that he can change the way we see and feel about ourselves. Take back your power ladies!!! When we waste our time in unhealthy relationships, it stagnates our growth when it comes to relationships. We find ourselves shutting down. We cannot grow if we are dormant. Had I removed myself from this relationship when I realized that he was not good for me, I could have spent more time working on me, my dreams, goals, which would have put me in a position to meet someone who could have helped me grow, a partnership verses a disaster-ship. My point is time is valuable & precious, use it wisely.

EXCUSES WE MAKE TO STAY IN UNHEALTHY RELATIONSHIPS:

1. I cannot pay my rent/bills without his help
2. I don't want my kids to be without a father/man in the house
3. We have been together for years; I don't want to start over
4. No man is perfect, so what's the sense of leaving
5. I can change him
6. The other woman will get tired before I do
7. He has great sex; I won't find that anywhere else
8. It will hurt too bad if I leave
9. I'm afraid that he might fight/hurt me if I try to leave
10. He might marry another woman if I leave him
11. I love him

When you're done making all these excuses ask yourself how valuable is your time?

1. Downsize, and get what you can afford on you own

2. He will always be their father, if he is mature, he will always be there to raise his kid(s) and co-parent without you all being in an unhealthy relationship

3. History with someone does not make you happy. You should rather take a risk to be with someone who will value you and do whatever it takes to add to your happiness & help you grow. Happiness is from within, people shouldn't be able to make you happy, but surely should add to it. Happiness over history!!!

4. Not being perfect is not an excuse to mistreat people. Leaving makes lots of sense if you are unhappy, especially if you are being mistreated in front of your kid(s)

5. Listen to K-Michelle's song "Can't Raise a Man" the best song ever, I couldn't have said it better myself.

6. Some women don't get tired, they brainwash themselves into thinking that coming second, or whatever place they come in is okay. Especially when there are benefits to it, like sex, secret dates, vacations, false promises, gifts, money, etc.

7. Trust me, great sex is better when you're being treated well, and intimacy is involved

8. What's the difference? It's hurting you to stay.

9. Get the police involved if you have to or supportive family/brothers

10. Soooooo!!!!!!!!!!!!! Farewell and good riddance! I have turned down a proposal before, although I made bad choices in men, I knew that I wanted a healthy marriage ordained by God. It would not be wise to except a proposal from a man who's showing clear signs of immaturity, cheating, not helping financially, non-supportive, etc.

11. Love yourself more!

I want to thank all the men who I crossed paths with in my dating era, for helping to mold me into the amazing woman that I am today. Some were lessons, some blessings, either way, I learned something from you all.

T.D. - Father of my first-born son, taught me to not ignore the signs, don't make excuses to stay, leave, get out!!! Showed me that everybody doesn't mature over time, people are okay with who they are if they think there is nothing wrong with them. (CANCER)

M. E. - A good man & friend, taught me that maturity has nothing to do with age, because even at a young age he was very mature. Kudos to his parents, they raised him well. (AQUARIUS)

D.B. - He was good to me, but I had other interest, later married his high school love. Taught me that men have feelings too. (PISCES)

U.S. - He was good to me, romantic, lots of fun, intelligent, well rounded hustler, but had issues with telling the truth, as lots of men his age did. He taught me to take care of myself before trying to take care of the rest of the world and to call people out when being untruthful so that they take accountability. (SAGITTARIUS)

W.S.-Short term relationship, showed me that even men need healing. (VIRGO)

T.H. - These initials do not stand for Tommy Hilfiger Lol. He showed me that a man will play games as long as you allow him to stay in the game. Later married the mother of his child. (SCORPIO-MY BIRTHDAY TWIN)

R.B. - Father of my second born son, later matured. We are co-parenting our 14-year-old, whom he has always taken care of financially. He taught me that you cannot raise a man and just because you love someone does not mean it is meant for you all to be together. A man will mature in due time with life's lessons, not with force or time wasted. He taught me that learned behavior is real because he wanted to live the lifestyle that he saw while he was growing up. (CAPRICORN)

T.M. - Good person with a big heart, good friend, and good father to his daughter, and a good son from what I could tell. He taught me that even men can be scarred. (CANCER)

Jeffrey O. Green

He showed me that shivery wasn't dead, that a man should still open doors for you, pull out your chair, and give you his jacket when you are cold. He walked on the outside of the street so that I was shielded & protected, that a man should add to your happiness, not destroy it. He was attentive, he made me feel special, he was supportive and he had my back. He showed me friendship within a relationship. Even when we were at odds, he still made sure I was okay. He showed me what a partnership was. He saw my beauty through my flaws.

He was slow to anger and has never put his hands on me, but to make me feel good. His words wrapped around me like a soft blanket-always soothing & warm. Either way, this relationship was truly a blessing. Our relationship taught me many things. The best lesson was not to allow love to make decisions for me. Sometimes you have to think outside of love to make sure you are making the right decisions for you. Love can make us selfish sometimes if we are not careful. Sometimes choosing the friendship over the relationship is not always a bad idea. This is the choice we made for a few reasons. We had a healthy relationship and a healthy breakup. This is a perfect example of everybody you love is not intended to be for a lifetime, even healthy-good relationships can be for a season. Learn the difference before wasting too much of your time. (LIBRA)

Ladies please do a **qualification check** on men before you allow them in your life and/or around your kids.

Have you ever heard the song "It Kills Me by Melanie Fiona?" Well here goes:

It Kills Me

Melanie Fiona

I've got trouble with my friends
Trouble in my life
Problems when you don't come home at night
but when you do you always start a fight
But I can't be alone, I need you to come on home
I know you messing around, but who the hell else is gonna
hold me down
Oh I gotta be out my mind to think it's gonna work this time
A part of me wants to leave, but the other side still believes
And it kills me to know how much I really love you
So much I wanna ooh ho oh to you hoo
Should I grab his cell, call this chic up
Start some shit and then hang up
Or should I be a lady
Ooh maybe cause I wanna have his babies

Oh yeah yeah cause I don't wanna be alone

I don't need to be on my own

But I love this man

but some things I just can't stand oh

I've gotta be out my mind

to…

I've gotta be out my mind

To think its gonna work this time

A part of me wants to leave but the other half still believes

And it kills me to know how much I really love you

So much I wanna ooh hoo oh, to you hoo ho

Should I pay him back to see how he'll react,

To see if he'll react to my love, my love

Ooh I've gotta be out my mind

To think it's gonna work this time

A part of me wants to leave

But the other side still believes

And it kills me to know how much

I really love you

So much I wanna oh ho to you ho ho

And it kills me (kills me)

To know how much

I really love you (how much, how much I love you)

So much I wanna oh ho to you ho ho

Songwriters: Leon L N Carr / Earl Shuman / Robert Littlejohn Jr / Andrea Martin

It Kills Me lyrics © Sony/ATV Music Publishing LLC, Warner/Chappell Music, Inc., Universal Music Publishing Group, Music Sales Corporation

(I am not claiming any rights to these lyrics; they are used as lesson teaching only)

Ladies lets focus on the words in **BOLD,** why do we allow this? Although these are lyrics from a song, we are very aware that this happens all around us with women we know or have heard of. Even us personally. Why can't we control our emotions enough to say enough is enough? Why are we so afraid to be alone? Why don't we value and love ourselves enough to recognize that this is not the way love should be or feel? My answer is; because we were not taught what healthy relationships should be like.

I recommend reading a book titled: Where Are Your Standards?

By: Debra Clifton-Mitchell, best-selling author.

I wish I had met her when I was younger.

Healthy relationships are more important than we know, because when we are in toxic/unhealthy relationships, it affects the people around us, especially our children. Have you ever yelled at your child because you were angry or hurt about something your boyfriend/man did to you? Do you know that our children can feel our tension and sadness even when they are in our womb?

While the body works on its own to heal physical damage like cuts and bruises, emotional wounds are much more complex to heal. Healing emotional scars requires consciousness and intentionality and that is not easy. My intentions are not to bash men, or claim that all men are bad, but to help you understand the importance of healthy relationships and choosing your partner wisely. He may one day be your husband, or father of your child, and for those reasons you do not want to make a bad choice.

Ladies let's start today making better choices in men. Some women think if I put up with him long enough he will eventually change. That is sometimes true. Some men do mature and change their ways, but after all the mistreatment, hurt, heartbreak, disrespect, will your love for him still be the same? Will those butterflies in your stomach still flutter or have they turned into moths? Will it be worth the time you have invested in him? Ask yourself these questions before you waste time that you can't get back.

Reflection:

_____

_____

_____

_____

_____

_____

_____

_____

_____

_____

_____

_____

_____

_____

_____

_____

_____

JOURNEY 5

Love vs. Dickmatized

❧

Ladies, do we know the difference? Would we stay in toxic relationships as long as we do if the sex was not good? To be honest, I don't believe most women would. The reason that I am comfortable making this statement is because we stay in relationships after things has drastically changed to the point where we are no longer happy, but we are tolerating men even though they cheat and mistreat us. What other reason do we stay?

I believe that many reasons we waste so much time in relationships is because of great sex, fear of being alone, or just to be able to say we got somebody. We need to realize that being alone is not a bad thing. Take time to love and heal yourself. Simple things like walks in the park, taking yourself on a movie date, a stay-cation, reading, loving yourself, getting to know yourself, are all parts of healing. Find ways to add to yourself by learning a new skill, returning to school, taking a class on something that interests you, starting a new hobby, starting a small business, or volunteering at a charity of interest. Always focus on bettering yourself. If we spent more time doing that vs. running up behind a good penis, we would add value to ourselves, which will attract better men. Ladies wasting time causes regrets. You will find yourself saying things like: I wish I could get a do-over, if only I knew then what I know now. I wish I had listened to my gut/intuition, if I had left after the first time he cheated, or showed signs that he was a waste of time. I should have finished college, or started my own business. Ladies time is precious, don't waste a second of it. Sometimes sex is a distraction and detours us from what is important.

I have been around women who continue to sleep with their child's father even though he is not spending time with, or financially helping with the child, because of good sex. Imagine what that does to the child when they see their father walk pass them to go into your bedroom and then don't see him again or have any other interaction with him other than seeing him stop by to have sex with you. Kids are very smart & observant. What do you think that does to the child? How they look at you after hearing you complain that the father is not involved in the kid's life or helping take care of them. Psychology studies show that when a child sees their mother who they love & respect, allowing a man to hit or mistreat her, loses respect for his or her mother.

I know women who have been burned (STD's) during sex, but continues to have sex with men without protection because they are dickmatized. H.I.V. numbers continue to rise according to the Chicago health Department. Can sex really be that good that we're willing to risk our health? Are you all aware that too many STD's, especially untreated ones, can cause health problems or cause you to become barren (not able to have kids), is sex worth all of this? No! Please understand the difference between Love & Lust/Dickmatized:

Love: Love is patient, love is kind. It does not envy, it does not boast, it is not proud. It does not dishonor others, it is not self-seeking, it is not easily angered, it keeps no record of wrongs. Love does not delight in evil, but rejoices with the truth. It always protects, always trusts, always hopes, always perseveres. Most importantly- it never hurts!

Dickmatized: When the dick is so good that you start catching feelings for the guy, when really you are just catching feelings for the dick; to be obsessed with penis.

Ladies do not tolerate mistreatment in exchange for good sex. Our bodies are temples and should be treated as such. Remember that all spirits are not good ones, so be careful who you allow in your bed, your space, and your life. Sex is a sacred exchange, an energy trade. Be careful who you share yourself with. The saying, one night of pleasure can lead to a lifetime of pain, is very true with H.I.V. & other incurable diseases that are so rampant.

Temporary pleasure is not worth a lifetime of pain!!!

JOURNEY 6

The Apple Doesn't Fall Too Far from the Tree

❦

Meaning; You have similar characteristics or habits of one or both parents. In psychology it means; learned behavior. There are four types of parenting styles:

1. **Authoritarian parenting:** Believing that a child should be seen and not heard. Talking at a child instead of to him/her.

2. **Authoritative parenting:** The parent makes an effort to maintain a healthy relationship with the child. Explains the reasons behind the rules.

3. **Permissive parenting:** Set rules, but rarely enforces them. There are no consequences behind the child's negative behavior.

4. **Uninvolved parent**: Parent is not communicating with the child about school, homework, social life, etc. The parent does not know the child's whereabouts, or who they are hanging out with. Don't spend much time with the child. Always focused on work, social life, and a man/relationship more than the child

If you are a parent, which parenting style do you display? Be honest with yourself. Well, my mother was the authoritarian, permissive, and uninvolved parent. I don't hold it against her because she displayed what she was taught or observed as a child and young adult. It is a cycle that needs to be broken before our children have to suffer because of it. The way I was raised and what I observed growing up, plays a role in how I am as an adult. Being raised by parents who did not instill confidence in me or was not very knowledgeable caused delayed learning and affected my decision making.

When you lack proper education and have been raised by parents who didn't give you the skills needed to prepare you for life, it's like playing a game without all the pieces. That does not mean that you cannot win the game, it just means it will be much harder.

My mother made sure we had somewhere to live, which included moving a lot. We had food to eat, clean clothing, and went to school every day, the basics, which I am grateful for. I also observed that settling was okay, wasting time on men who did not have good qualities was normal, that mediocracy was okay, that living check to check was normal, and depending on government assistance while allowing it to stagnate you was normal.

I take accountability for my mistakes and bad decisions, but I know for a fact that knowledge is power, education is important, common sense is needed for critical thinking, financial education is a must, and last but very importantly, love & support is needed for healthy growth.

Ladies, make sure your parenting skills is promoting healthy growth & development. How you teach, discipline, raise, and interact with your child can make a grave (serious) difference in how they live their lives as adults. Parenting does not come with a handbook but make every effort to be the best parent you can be so that your kids won't have to suffer because of bad parenting, or to put it in a positive light, I will call it unknowledgeable parenting.

Taking early childhood education & psychology classes, later observing healthy relationships between other parents and their children, and listening to Joel Osteen is what helped me with parenting. I am still learning to this day the importance of good parenting. How to allow my kids to speak their mind and express themselves, but not be disrespectful, to understand that parenting does not come with a guide book, and I don't know everything, nor will I do everything right, but I will always do my best. Also, that it's okay to show emotions, but not be weak, to be confident and have self-esteem, but not be arrogant, to set goals, and complete them.

I love my kids, as I'm sure all mothers do, but to show them how much we really love them, is to be the best parents we can be and never stop learning, so that you can teach them. Discipline is love, conversations is love, providing them with the tools they need to be successful is love, knowing their whereabouts is love, to be their parent and not their friend is love.

Let me share some history about my mother to show you that learned behavior is real and how history can repeat itself if we don't break the chains. My mother dropped out of high school, I did as well, although for different reasons. She has cognitive issues/learning disability so do I. A.D.D. is a real disorder and stands for Attention Deficit Disorder. It makes it hard to stay focused, hard to remember & retain information, and issues comprehending to some things. It could simply be a lack of education from schools or parents. I'm not a scientist so I can only speak on my experience with what they diagnosed as A.D.D.

I will not and have not allowed this to affect me or detour me, but the symptoms are real no matter the cause.

She started dating at age 15, so did I? My mother had me at age 19, I had my child at age 19 as well. My mother stayed in relationships for long lengths of time, as I did, without the thought or mention of marriage. She was with my dad, **Charles E. Looney**- (Deceased in 2008) her first boyfriend for

15 years, and she took a short break, than have now been with my sister's dad for 33 years. She has always gave more of herself then people deserve, as I've done as well. She made excuses for her kids and defended them when she should have been teaching them accountability, as I did. Instead of being a tool, she was a crutch, as I had learned to be. Proud to say I have learned and no longer follow that path.

My siblings are Alex C. Streeter, Charles E. Streeter (Maria Basulto-Streeter-Sister-in-law), Ron Streeter, & finally I got a little sister, Tracy L. Streeter. We are all very close and get alone well. We are all loving, supportive, and have a strong bond. When I see family members who are not close or supportive of one another it is so surprising to me, because I cannot imagine family not being close. I thought that was the sole purpose of a family. I guess I was wrong, because I've seen families feud and fight like strangers.

Here are the areas where I broke the cycle:

I returned to school to get my G.E.D, then went on to college. I have had several jobs, probably more than I should have, but

I worked because I knew I wanted my own money and more for my kids. I taught myself financial literacy since the schools or my parents didn't/couldn't teach it to me. I stopped wasting time in unhealthy relationships. I stopped giving so much of myself to the point where I was drained/depleted, especially to people who didn't deserve it. I learned to be a tool for my kids & others and not a crutch, they now stand on their own two feet, but I support them always. I am no longer okay with just being okay. I am striving to be the best I can be so that I can have the desires of my heart and help my kids have the chances in life they deserve. My goal is to leave them with knowledge that they will hopefully apply and generational wealth that they will not squander.

Let your kids know that they were born for a special purpose. In the words of journalist William Hodding Carter "There are only two things we can hope to give our children:

One is roots, Children who know they are loved unconditionally are children with roots. Consequently, they are able to stand up to whatever life throws at them.

Second is wings, by the same token, when you instill in your children a sense of self-confidence and encourage them to dream, you are giving them wings. Any time children are given the will to win, they are already halfway to success, but if you allow them to grow up without it, they are already halfway to failure. As a parent you must demonstrate faith in your children so that they have faith in themselves. Every child has within them a God-given seed of greatness and when you let them know that you believe in them- you are watering that seed and giving them a chance to grow.

When you constantly criticize kids, they grow up to be negative, self-doubting and fearful, but when you believe in them and assume they will do well, they will go the extra mile by trying to live up to your expectations. It is your faith in them that creates the environment in which they learn to fly! Give them money, they will spend it, give them resources, they will squander them, but give them faith in God and in themselves, chances are, they will excel at whatever they do.

The apple doesn't fall too far from the tree implies that good, bad, successful, mediocre, smart, unintelligent, married, unmarried, etc., usually strong traits from the parent(s) are transferred from the parent(s) and instilled in the child(ren). My mother did not instill confidence in me. I'm sure it was not on purpose, so I do not fault her. I can't remember her ever saying "You can be whatever you want to be if you apply yourself." She didn't sit down with me to discuss school, college, plans for the future, what a healthy relationship should look or feel like, but again, I don't blame her because she was never taught, and neither did her mom have those conversations with her. All my teachings were about survival, so now I will unteach to reteach myself how to live and do it in abundance. You should try this as well.

The worst memory I had as a young adult (age 19) was our living situation. We lived in a court way building on Westend & Lamon in Chicago, IL. which is now torn down. The landlord ran off with the rents and security deposits knowing that the building was in foreclosure. Most people moved out right away because they had jobs and were prepared financially. My mom was on welfare and had to wait on government assistance to be able to have rent for our next move. Well the move was further delayed due to a home invasion robbery where three men came in and took the money my mom had saved. It was odd that they knew exactly where the money was. Found out later that my female cousin Vee allegedly had us set up according to word on the street. This broke my mother's heart since she had loaned her money, which is how she had knowledge of my mom's hiding spot. I was pregnant and near my due date at the time, so while everyone else was ordered to get down on the floor, I was allowed to sit in a chair, which is how I got to see the specific details about the men which later led to their arrest.

Three days later I had a healthy baby boy 7/13/1991, 6lbs. 9oz. I knew I had to do something. The water went off and we had to get water from a nearby water hydrant and purchase jugs of water from the store. My brothers and male cousin would dump the feces from the toilet at night when it was full so that we could use the toilet. Two weeks after he was born I moved in with a friend. I cried myself to sleep at night knowing that my newborn was living in these conditions but glad that he did not know, understand, or was not affected by it (that I know of) because I made sure he was well taken care of. I vowed that I would work hard so that my child would never have to experience such living situations.

I am also very grateful that I missed the peer pressure of drug and alcohol abuse although my family didn't. My mom drinks lots of beer and because it is not hard alcohol, she will not accept the fact that it is still poisoning her system. Drinking too much beer, or any other type of alcohol, is bad for you. "Heavy alcohol consumption wipes out any health benefit and increases risk of liver cancer, cirrhosis, alcoholism, and obesity. My brothers have indulged in pcp, heroin, ecstasy, alcohol, nicotine, etc. These things can cause major mental and health issues, but I am grateful to say that with love, support, the wrecking of my nerves, and lots of prayer, they have overcome it. I love my family unconditionally, neither of us is better than, or better off than the other. We are all in this family thing together. Family is important. God didn't make a mistake with the family he chose for you. Try to see the best in one another and always genuinely love and support one another.

We are wonderfully made and not a mistake. It does not matter what type of family you were born into; it was not an error. Did you know you started out as a single cell and within that cell was enough DNA to hold the equivalent of 1,000 volumes of blueprints? As well as, DNA determines the color of your hair and eyes, shape of your nose, and the size of your ring finger? Did you know that nobody has your same laugh or fingerprints, the same sparkle in your eye, or looks at things the way you do? You are an original and should feel special. You are a masterpiece designed by a divine artist.

Statements parents should not live by:

- I break myself for my kids!

If you are speaking about material things and not for generational wealth, you need to rethink your parenting goals. There is nothing wrong with buying your kids nice things, but to break yourself is not a good idea.

- I allow my minor daughters' boyfriend/father of her child(ren) to sleep over nights so that she will not have to sneak around with him!

As the adult and parent, a minor or unmarried child should not have permission to shack or lay up with a boy/man in her mother/parents house.

- I allow my kids to smoke weed/indulge in drugs & alcohol in my presence so that they will not do it with strangers or in public!

Bad decision and a form of disrespect. If they use or abuse drugs, trust that most kids will do it anywhere with anybody. Do not subject yourself to that type of disrespect as a parent. There should always be boundaries between parents and children.

- I do not want my child to work and go to school!

This is reasonable, but don't limit your child. As long as they are not getting failing grades and over exerting themselves, they should get a taste of the real world and learn to fend for and take care of themselves with your support.

- It is okay for my daughter to be sexually active/ have a child at a young age because I did, babies are a blessing.

Babies are a blessing when you are mentally & financially stable to take care of them. Kids raising babies does not have a good turn out most times. Of course having supportive parents who is willing to help a minor raise a child helps, but how many parents are willing to do so? Our kids doing what we did doesn't make it right. We want to limit their regrets as much as possible.

- I cannot stop my sons from selling narcotics because that is what they saw growing up!

We should have been more careful with what we allowed our kids to see while growing up, but that is no excuse to be okay with it.

- It is okay for my child to live off government assistance!

This is not what we should be teaching our kids. Of course if they fall on hard times it's okay for temporary assistance, but should not be taught the mindset that government assistance is good to live on, especially since it is not guaranteed long-term.

- It is okay for my young children to be around during adult conversation, they don't understand what is being talked about.

The saying that kids brains are like sponges at as early as 2 years old is very true. Take heed!

- I give my kids cough syrup or beer to help them go to sleep, either because I am tired of being bothered, they will not stop crying, or I want to go hangout with friends to mingle or party.

If it is harmful to us as adults, imagine what it does to a baby or school aged children. It does horrible things to the kidney & liver.

- I am going to defend my kids no matter what they do!

You should protect your kids at all times, but defending them when they are wrong is teaching them not to take accountability for their actions. This will have consequences that affect them as adults.

THERE SHOULD BE NO LOVE OR BOND STRONGER THAN THE ONE YOU HAVE WITH FAMILY.

FAMILY FIRST!!!

Consider this chapter Parenting 101

Assets vs. Liabilities

❦

This is pretty simple. Assets add to your money or income, liabilities subtract from it. Keep this in mind and you will realize how it makes living simpler and less financially stressful. Let's look over some examples of both:

Assets:

1. Cash

2. Land

3. Rental property

4. Equity in a home

5. Stock (but can be a risk)

6. Marketable Securities

7. Financial Support System

Liabilities:

1. Cars (w/car note)

2. Debt

3. Loans

4. Law Suits against you

5. Mortgage

6. Overdraft fees

7. Hinders instead of helpers

Now let us talk about how people can add to us, or take away from us. We should always make sure people around us are adding to us and not subtracting, especially when it comes to friendships and relationships.

Friendship: A state of mutual trust & support, an unbreakable bond.

We can sometimes use this word lightly, assuming that everybody we are cool with is our friend. Not true! I have friends on different levels and from all walks of life. I take friendship very seriously. I value true friendship and am very loyal to it. You will never hear about me sleeping with my friends' man or husband, with the excuse, shit happens. There has never been a case where I didn't support my friends in any way that I could. I have friends who I feel comfortable talking to about anything. No matter how good, bad, ugly, embarrassing, or deep it is. I have friends who support me in all things. They don't care what it is, what it is for, or what it is about. They have my back and go above and beyond to support the cause whatever it may be.

I have history friends, we have been friend for 20+ years, so we just hold on to that, even though the friendship has kind of took a turn, not for the worse, just at a standstill. I have growth friends, who has taught me things, who has taken me to the next level in my life, they keep it real with me to help me, not to hurt me. I have friends who has not mastered the true meaning of friendship, but has good intentions. I Love them all.

I have friends who make 6 figures yearly, friends who are unemployed, & friends who are in the class of the working poor. Friends who has never drank or indulged in drugs, but

I also have friends whom I have helped overcome heroin addiction, alcohol abuse, depression, etc. I love them all. I don't judge a book by its cover. We all have a story behind the reason we are who we have become and reasons that we act or respond the way we do. You should not expect more than you are willing to give. Always be the best friend that you can be. I have great friends, because I display great friendship. You usually attract people who are similar to you. If you feel like you have friends who are not giving you their all, or going above and beyond for you, maybe you should think about what type of friend you are and consider that may be the reason you are not getting the help and response you want from your friends.

I say choose your friends wisely, because just like a relationship with the opposite sex, betrayal from friendship can hurt and scar you just like a bad relationship. I have learned that some people can only be happy for you if they are happy for themselves. They are only proud of you if they have accomplishments to be proud of. They are happy for your new relationship or husband only if they are in a happy union themselves. Some people have a hardened heart for many reasons and it takes lots of love & patience to soften it, but for some, you just have to let them go.

I want friends who are always happy for me and cheering for me no matter what their situation is. Sometimes you have to be stern and give your friends tough love, like your children. You have to literally tell people about themselves and it will either make them mad at you, resent you, or it will make them recognize the areas in which they need to do better. They will straighten up their act and you all can carry on with a healthy friendship. Choosing your friends wisely is important because they should be an asset in your life, not a liability! My friends are acknowledged below:

Chante Martin: Friendship Est. in 1992-Always supportive & uplifting, taught me to look at life with the cup half full, instead of half empty. She is a really special friend-like a sister. There is not enough words that can explain her friendship and how close we are.

Wanda (Latrice) Hudson: Friendship Est. in 2008–Very supportive, giving, goes above & beyond for friends.

Considerate, pays attention to detail in friendship, loyal. She taught me not to judge a book by its cover and that friends do not always need preaching to, or to be advised on what to do, but sometimes just needs a listening ear. Her type of friendship is rare and hard to come by.

Catherine Thompson: Friendship Est. in 2008-Empowering, very supportive, resilient. She taught me the importance of preparation, one of the best teachings of my life. (step-cousin)

Dana Mitchell: Friendship Est. in 1995-Supportive, my ride or die friend. Always there when I need her. Taught me that friendship is not perfect, to forgive even if it has not been requested, to embrace friendship, even with its flaws.

Dr. Catherine Eason: My mentor-friendship Est. in 2009-Supportive, encouraging, resourceful, inspired me to go to college. She also supported me financially so that I can return to college. She taught me that I can do anything if I believe in myself.

Ladonna Cannon: Spiritual friendship Est. in 2011-Good energy and uplifting, taught me to forgive myself and mean it when I say it. Her words of advice and encouragement helped me to release the toxins of regret.

Andrea Mitchell: BFF-Friendship Est. in 1992-Loyal, supportive, fun-loving, taught me that friendship won't always balance. She can take constructive criticism and always putting forth the effort to be the best friend she can be.

Latasha Haggard: God-sister-Friendship Est. in 1990-Loyal, sincere, supported me through some emotional times in my life. Taught me that we do not all grow at the same pace, but will get to exactly where we need to be.

Felice Lewis: Friendship Est. in 2010-My A-1, we clicked on day 1, loyal, never switches up. The rule no new friends does not apply to her. She taught me strength through hers and that nothing is ever as bad as it seems.

Edie (Bay-Bay) McKnight: Friendship Est. in 1985-My fun childhood friend, supportive, was there during my second baptism.

Latanesha (Honhon) Sheley: Friendship Est. in 1995-Always had my back, taught me to never depend solely on a man, to always secure myself. She said something that stuck with me that taught me to carry myself as a God-fearing woman so that when others looked at me, they saw the difference between worldly and the fruit of the spirit. She stated "Why should I go to church, when the people who do, live their life just as I do, so what is the difference?" She had a point, but what I should have said was, "We are all a work in progress and all need to hear the word of God to guide us in our everyday lives with the help of the Holy Spirit."

Tonya Day: Friendship Est. in 1992-Taught me that although friends may grow apart, it does not change the fact that a friendship once existed.

Leslie (Toni) Wolfe: (Deceased) Friendship Est. in 1985-Heart of gold, she taught me things that I needed to know as a girl transitioning into womanhood. She was always there for me. I miss her dearly. She taught me to take nothing for granted and no matter how sad or bad things can sometimes be in this life, that there is always something to be grateful for.

Stephanie Velez: Friendship Est. in 2012- My resourceful, resilient friend. She is supportive and easy to talk to.

My girl cousins were my first friends: **Laketia, Doretha, Wanda, Demetria, Twania, Shawanna, & Sabrina-Spiritual connection & unbreakable bond, Scorpio cousins, intense & emotional, so we understand each other,**

Relationship: An intimate partnership where two people choose to date openly. You will be able to tell the difference through common sense, and-or intuition, if a man is a liability or an asset in your life. You should also know the difference between constructive criticism and being put down. If you get the two confused, you will think a man is not good for you, when he really is. If you are defensive, you can't tell if he is saying things to help you, or hurt you. Example: If he says: "You should return to school to get your diploma or degree, you're so smart, I support you." That's not a put down, or him trying to say you are beneath him because you don't have those things. He is simply showing you he wants the best for you and that he believes in you. If he says: "You so stupid and dumb, you need to go back to school, or if you mention returning to school and he says: "You are too old, or too stupid to go back to school." This proves that he is an insecure man who wants to stagnate you, out of fear that you will do better and move on without him.

People who add to your life and not subtract from it are clear examples of an asset. A person/man who just take, take, take, is clearly a liability. If you work every day and a man stays home, lives with you, or should I say "lives on you," because he is not contributing. If he drives your car, drop you off at work, don't pick you up on time, because he is hanging out all day, spending your money, but not making any, not helping with rent/bills, household supplies, food, not helping you grow financially, he is surely a liability. If you have a child or children together and he is not providing for his biological child, that is a major problem. Ladies, again, choose your friends and men wisely. Everybody that we allow into our lives can either add to us, or take away from us.

Do not allow people to take from you until there is nothing left!!!

Healthy relationships are very important, not just with the opposite sex, but with your children, family members and friends as well. Always be an asset in each other lives, this is so needed in relationships.

JOURNEY 8

Credit Check

L et's talk about credit and how it can affect your life in many ways, even in relationships. If you don't do a credit check on people, it could have a negative impact on your life. Let's talk about the credit expectancy of America.

Poor Credit	Fair Credit	Good Credit	Excellent Credit
300-579	580-669	670-740	741-850

Having a good credit score is very important if you cannot, or choose not to pay for everything in full. I was never taught on the importance of credit as a young adult, so I had to learn the hard way. I will share some personal reasons with you on how my credit was destroyed in hopes that you will not make the same mistakes as I did. My first time checking my credit was at age 28. My score was 385.

The average FICO score in America is 695 and the average Vantage score stands at 673. Currently, Fair Isaac Corp's FICO score and Vantage are two of the most widely used scoring models in the country according to credit.com. Both models range between 300 and 850 the higher the score, the better.

I never knew that if I wanted to purchase a home, new car, rental property, boat, timeshare, anything of value that was out of my budget, or income bracket, that I would need to apply for credit and approval would be based on my credit history, score, & debt to income ratio. It started when I wanted a new-beautiful bedroom set that I could not afford and needed a cosigner. My gut warned me, if you can't afford to buy it, you don't need it, but of course, I wanted what I wanted, so I applied for credit, and was **Denied!!!** No creditor would've given me a line of credit with a credit score as low as mine. Out of pity, a friend of mine co-signed for a $2500.00 credit card. If I had patience, and financial sense, I could have bought the set by saving for it, and not owed Harlem Furniture a dime, or ruined my friend's credit.

After my friend co-signed, I was approved and my items arrived in 3 business days. I was so excited to have this pretty, comfortable bedroom set. I had never had a bedroom set in my life, just always had a bed to sleep on and maybe a hand-me down dresser. Of course, like anything, it got old and I got bored with it, but the monthly bill didn't stop coming. After a while I was in-between jobs and had lacked discipline. I stop paying on the line of credit, not even consciously thinking that this would affect my friend.

After I realized how it affected her credit score, I felt horrible. Here are 10 reasons not to co-sign:

1. Co-signing a loan is high risk-low reward.
2. The lender will sue you first if payments are not made.
3. The person you help will be happy, but you will have a lot to lose.
4. Co-signing a loan can destroy friendships and family relationships if the loan is not paid.
5. You are 100 percent liable on a loan that could be a significant amount.

6. You could face tax consequences from co-signing a loan if the debt is settled.

7. Co-signing a loan could make approval of a loan you might need impossible.

8. You may need to sue the other responsible party if payments are not made and you get sued.

9. You have to be organized enough to keep track of the payments when co-signing, and be financially prepared to pay when the account own can't, or choose not to pay.

10. Last but surely not least, it is just a bad idea.

After what I put my friend through, I made a vow to never ask anyone to take on that type of responsibility again. Because I had no knowledge of how credit or co-signing worked, or that she would be responsible for my debt, I negatively affected her credit. I also made a vow that I would never co-sign for anyone. Well sometimes kindness can cause us to make bad decisions. I co-signed for a car for a family member, when she became ill and couldn't work, she couldn't keep up with the car note, which affected my credit. At the time I wasn't financially stable enough to take on the responsibility of paying her note, I was paying on my own car. My credit score dropped tremendously. All the discipline and hard work I put into building my credit score from 385 to 700 went down the drain, and caused me to start building again from scratch. I learned that it's okay to say "No, I am not financially stable enough to take such a risk for you."

Doing a credibility check on people you allow in your life is just as important as checking your credit. As I have learned, anybody that we allow to enter into our space, can have a negative or positive affect on the outcome of our lives, just like a credit score. More reasons that a man needs a credibility check, is because we need to be careful who we have kids by, for many reasons. Medical & mental illness, back child support, history of verbal & physical abuse, cheating, con-artist, manipulators laziness, criminal offenses, pedophiles, etc. All these things can have a negative impact on a child. We have to start taking relationships more serious ladies. It's more to a relationship than going out on fun dates and sex. The father being present in a child's life is very important and shouldn't be taken lightly. It is evident that we won't always marry and live happily ever after with the men we have a child with, but if we make better choices in men, co-parenting will be a breeze and is in the child's best interest.

Fathers play a role in every child's life that cannot be filled by others. This role can have a large impact on a child and help shape him or her into the person they become. Fathers, like mothers, are pillars in the development of a child's emotional well-being. Children look to their fathers to lay down the rules and enforce them. They also look to their fathers to provide a feeling of security, both physical and emotional. Children want to make their fathers proud and an involved father promotes inner growth and strength. Studies have shown that when fathers are affectionate and supportive, it greatly affects a child's cognitive and social development. It also instills an overall sense of well-being and self-confidence.

Young girls depend on their fathers for protection. A father shows his daughter what a good relationship with a man is like. If a father is loving and gentle, his daughter will look for those qualities in men when she is old enough to begin dating.

If a father is supportive, consistent, and stable, she will relate closely to men of the same traits.

Unlike girls who model their relationships with others based on their father's character, boys' model *themselves* after their father's character. Boys will seek approval from their fathers from a very young age. As human beings, we grow up by imitating the behavior of those around us; that is how we learn to function in the world. If a father is caring and treats people with respect, the young boy will grow up much the same. When a father is absent, young boys look to other male figures to set the "rules" for how to behave and survive in the world. Unfortunately, the male figure is not always a positive role model. This is why young boys/men join gangs to substitute for the father they didn't have. They need protection, money, survival skills, and a male figure to look up to, so they assume this is their only option. It's sad that they have easy access to gang members' verses mentors and positive leaders.

Decisions you make and time wasted on things or people can dictate the direction of your life. There are so many things that could cause us to wish we could have a do-over. Trust me, if I can help detour you from making the same mistakes that I did, I will. That is the goal of this book. If you have already made these mistakes, I am here to let you know it is not the end of your world. We do not get a do-over, but we do get another chance to learn from our mistakes and do better.

It is never too late to remove negative inquires from your credit report, or people from your life who can impact you in a negative way. Performing credit checks on your report & people are equally important sense they both can affect you.

Reflection:

Reborn @ Forty

❦

Butterfly Life Cycle

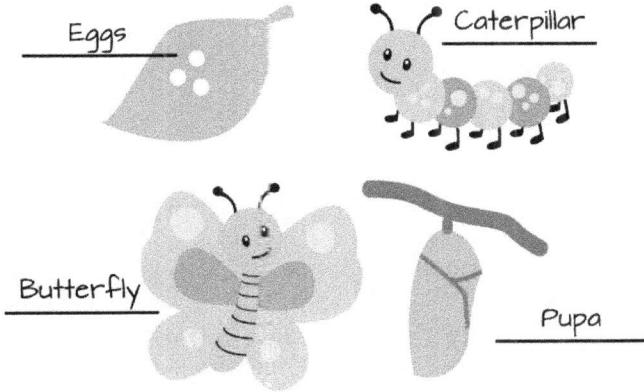

Eggs

Caterpillar

Butterfly

Pupa

I compare my life to a butterfly because of the stages it goes through and it's my favorite insect. The process as well as the colors are beautiful. At age forty something came over me that I've never felt at any other ages or stages of my life cycle. I had an epiphany! I felt reborn, different, mindset changed, my tolerance for unpleasant things, and people were very low. So many things became unacceptable. Although it is said we are adult women at age 18, I wasn't a mature adult until age 40.

The Egg: Age 0-18 Birth to young adult/Carefree.

The Caterpillar: 19-25 the feeding stage, in taking knowledge.

The Pupa: Age 26-39 Transition, shedding of old skin, starting to take life more seriously.

The Butterfly: 40+ Reproductive stage, recreate oneself, mentally & spiritually mature, magical, beautiful, a masterpiece.

My fascination with butterflies is unexplainable. I have tatts of butterflies. The stages and process of the butterfly is amazing, a work of art. God could not have created a more beautiful, intriguing creature/insect.

As I spoke about in the first paragraph, things & people became intolerable. I could no longer tolerate people taking my kindness for weakness, employers who didn't value me, unsupportive family & friends whom I've always supported, disloyal, dishonest friends, and men who were not ready for commitment. I made the decision to not settle in none of the areas in my life. I began to look for the deeper meaning of life. You try to understand why you are here and how you can make your life more meaningful.

I started looking for my path and seeking inner peace. My mind fully awakened at age forty. The alternative choice is to recognize the ego but not succumb to it, to allow it to find its place harmoniously within the whole. You continue your journey with humility and devotion. It is then that you are fully mature.

We are born into a material world where your life is dominated by your ego. You enter the world in a state of innocence and as long as you are healthy and have a loving family, you live in a world of joy and bliss, but as life goes on things become difficult, life is not as simple as it once was. Now you have to figure things out, you start to wonder how did I get here. I started feeling consumed by the demands of society telling me who and what I should be by a certain age, I couldn't take it ANYMORE, and it started to cause anxiety. I took control of my life! You can too.

I WAS REBORN @ AGE 40!!!

JOURNEY 10

No More Settling!!!

❧

After reflecting back on my life, I realized that I had settled in all the areas of my life. I never expected much from myself or others. I never demanded anything. I was okay with just being okay. I settled for surviving instead of living, for boyfriends & baby daddy's instead of a husband, for toxic relationships versus healthy ones. I settled for jobs that didn't value me or pay well instead of pursuing my passions and using the money from working to invest in myself. I settled for thinking I wasn't deserving or good enough because of my demographic status. I settled for poverty instead of success. I am done settling!!! I know that I am deserving of everything good and that nothing & nobody can stop me, but me. Ladies the decision is yours not to settle.

Here are 5 tips from psychology today, along with my own opinion of ways to avoid settling:

1. Stop rationalizing the poor behavior of others.

Do you frequently make excuses for others' mistreatment of you? "He had a bad day, that's why he's lashing out," or "She's had a hard life, that's why she expects so much of me." It matters if you don't have peace of mind in your relationships. Instead of rationalizing, try to speak directly to what hurts you. If the people you are close to can't hear you, or if they dismiss or invalidate you, and you accept that, you are settling for less than what you deserve.

2. Recognize that not getting what you want is not a personal curse.

You make yourself vulnerable to settling if you tell yourself that you are cursed by forces outside of your control when hardship or setbacks occur. That point of view concedes defeat. Life is sometimes unfair, but not always. Each time you try for something you want, wipe the slate clean. Otherwise you allow the bitterness of earlier disappointments (not forces outside of your control) to make you vulnerable to settling for less than you deserve and can achieve.

3. Recognize that being alone is not the same as being lonely.

Being alone does not mean you are flawed. If you cannot be alone, you will settle for lousy friendships and lovers just to find a diversion from <u>loneliness</u>. Accept being alone now, so you can be with someone better later.

4. Become use to expressing what you desire—and say it repeatedly.

No one gets what they want if they don't fully accept and recognize what they desire and communicate it to the people in their lives. Get in touch with what you want, big and small. Talk about it with friends, family, and acquaintances. Say it out loud. Put the universe on notice so support can come back to you.

5. Don't agree with what you don't want.

A huge part of settling is being a "yes man" woman. If you agree to things you don't really want, you are building a life that doesn't reflect your own needs and <u>identity</u>. When asked to do something, or even when you are asked what you want for dinner, allow yourself to pause and go inward. Ask yourself, "What do I want to eat?" "Do I want to do this?" or "What kind of work do I wish to do?" and then heed the answers.

Say it out loud: I deserve the best of everything!!! The best is the only thing worth settling for!!!

JOURNEY 11

Facetime/Self Awareness

❧

Self-awareness is conscious knowledge of one's own character, feelings, motives, & desires. I had to master this to learn who I really was. Self-awareness is really important. If you are not aware, you will not be conscious of which areas you need self-improvement, or how to better yourself as an individual. I thought I was a woman who had it all together until I realized I needed to evaluate myself. See the table below to learn more about self-awareness.

The Four Self-Awareness Archetypes

This 2x2 maps internal self-awareness (how well you know yourself) against external self-awareness (how well you understand how others see you).

	Low external self-awareness	High external self-awareness
High internal self-awareness	**INTROSPECTORS** They're clear on who they are but don't challenge their own views or search for blind spots by getting feedback from others. This can harm their relationships and limit their success.	**AWARE** They know who they are, what they want to accomplish, and seek out and value others' opinions. This is where leaders begin to fully realize the true benefits of self-awareness.
Low internal self-awareness	**SEEKERS** They don't yet know who they are, what they stand for, or how their teams see them. As a result, they might feel stuck or frustrated with their performance and relationships.	**PLEASERS** They can be so focused on appearing a certain way to others that they could be overlooking what matters to them. Over time, they tend to make choices that aren't in service of their own success and fulfillment.

SOURCE DR. TASHA EURICH   © HBR.ORG

I believe that I am an Introspector, moving into Aware. I limited my own success by not believing in myself, because I was not raised around successful people. It was not instilled in me. I was not raised with self-confidence, that plays a role in success. Self-awareness is not just about the outcome of success. You need to know your good side and bad side. Although we would like to believe that we're a 100% good, it is not true. I had to facetime myself, and say; "Self who are you?" What do you want out of life? What are your strengths and weaknesses? How can you be better in all the areas of your life? What do you need to stop, or start doing? I had to admit to myself that I needed to listen more and talk less. I had to realize that I did not comprehend to some things well. I know that the tone in my voice can sound harsh when I am irritated, or having a back & forth conversation that annoys me. I now know that I am protective and possessive when it comes to the people I love. (not in a dangerous controlling way) I shut down when my feelings are hurt, or somebody rubs me the wrong way. I love long and hard, but dislike a person easy if they do things that causes me not trust them. I made excuses for people because I wanted to see or believe the best about people. I crippled my kids by always running to their rescue and not being stern when I should have been. I was a crutch to everyone around me because of my kindness, and that I hated to see people struggle, but have now learned to be a tool. I learned that I had great potential and plans, but no follow through or execution. I learned that I talked myself out of things out of fear of failure. I learned that I made things harder than they actually were because of doubt. I learned that I was in my own way. Most importantly, I have learned that struggle builds character and usually makes a person more determined.

Doing a Facetime with myself has helped me become self-aware and is one of the best things I have ever done for me. Keep it real with yourselves and become a better you!

Reflection:

Balance

~⟋⟋~

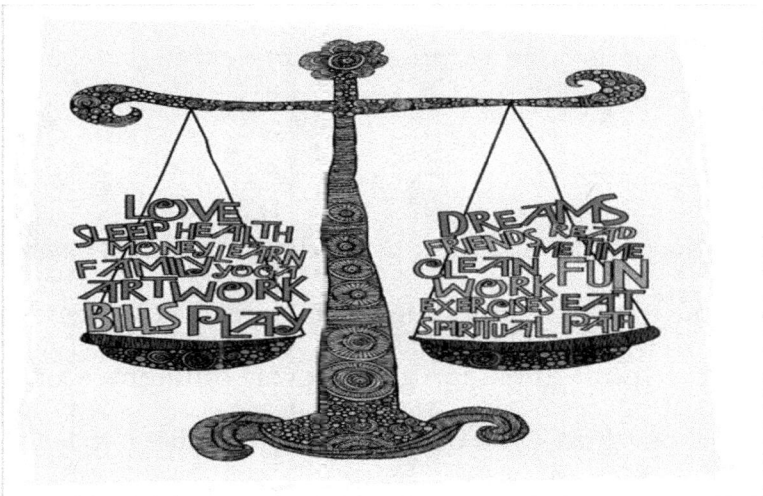

B alance: Without balance, life is bound to be chaotic. Meaning, in every area of your life you need to have the correct portions, not too much, not too little. When every area of your life has balance you won't be as stressed. I found myself trying to do everything at once trying to make up for lost time which is impossible. Once time is gone, that's just it.

I felt as if I had wasted so many years of my time settling in life, that I had to hurry up and cram life into a short time frame, which only overwhelmed me. The best thing to do is learn from wasted time, and move forward making better decisions, and to have good time management.

With all the things we have to balance, time management is a must. Most of us have all, or some of these things to balance:

Kids:

Always make time for your kid(s). I don't mean just be around them, I mean real quality time with interaction, conversation, teaching critical thinking, going over different scenarios, talking about things you don't want them to have to learn the hard way, or from somebody who will give them the wrong teachings & advice.

Family:

We may not always be close with everybody in our family for whatever the reason, but spending time and checking on family members is vital. You never know what people are going through and how one visit, or call can brighten their day.

Friends:

Choose friends wisely and be the friend that you want people to be in return. Spending time and enjoying friendship is important. Real friendship should be valued. You don't have to see your friends everyday to consider yourselves friends. Never judge them, but always be real with them.

Relationship/Marriage:

If you have chosen your partner wisely, time spent together will be enjoyable, not annoying.

Go on date nights, communicate openly & honestly. You shouldn't be under each other all day-everyday to feel secure, time apart is okay. Whether it be for work, hanging out with old friends, travel for business/vacations/retreats, etc. More importantly, trust, communication, support, compromise, and patience are mandatory in relationships/marriage.

School:

Education is important, so is study time. Make sure to spend enough time focusing on this to complete the courses needed to do what you are passionate about, and also be educated on it.

Work:

Use jobs as stepping stones, as well as, to make money work for you. It is unwise to spend your entire life working for money. Get in practice of saving and learn to invest your money. Get the skills you need for future endeavors. Don't allow work to consume you. Always balance it so that you're not stressed. Jobs can and will replace you in a heartbeat, so make sure your health is your top priority. Work is a place where you make money for everyday living and hopefully, you're able to advance and will be valued by the company you work for.

Hobbies/Extra curriculum activities:

So needed!!! Make time to do something you enjoy. I love reading & volleyball.

Clubbing/Partying:

If you can do this in a safe environment, by all means, get your party on. Don't allow anybody to make you believe you're too young or old to enjoy yourself. Balance it out though, because too much of it can be bad for you. If you drink, remember that you are a lady and should act as such. Never leave your drink unattended, even around people you think you can trust.

Exercise:

This should be a lifestyle, doesn't have to be overly excessive, but much needed for good health and also to relieve stress.

Meditation/Spiritual time: I didn't realize how important this was until age 40. We are around energies all day, some good, some bad, so equip yourself with meditation, prayer, yoga, spiritual readings like the bible, or daily bread pamphlets. To be at peace is the best part of life.

T.V. time: Depending on what you're watching, this should be in very small portions, even with the news. We want to be aware of what's going on in the world, but not so much of it that it's depressing, or overwhelming, as I have experienced in the past. Time is valuable/precious! Spend it on things that matter, things that can help you grow.

The importance of a balanced life, and maintaining it, is becoming increasingly more important for your personal health and well-being in a fast-paced, modern world. Sustaining a balanced diet, alongside personal fitness, can help improve and stabilize overall health and wellbeing. It is crucial that you have balance.

It is far too easy to think that you are doing everything wrong, and it is even easier to scroll through Instagram or Facebook and compare yourself to others that seem to live the perfect lifestyle. The key point here is; not to be hard on yourselves, stay in your own lane, everyone has their own journey to take. Having a balanced life doesn't happen overnight, but each little change we make is a step in the right direction. If we get lost and take the wrong path, it is not the end of the road, we just need to carry on, it is part of the journey. Keep it simple, and be kind to yourself.

JOURNEY 13

Saying Goodbye to the Past Forever!

❧

Kudos to those who can just pick up the shattered pieces of their past and rebuild. They move forward without ever looking back. For some people, getting over their past can be really difficult, especially when it includes trauma, pain, & regret. Living in the past is dangerous and causes stress, which can be physically & mentally unhealthy.

When we are stressed our immune system's ability to fight off antigens is reduced. This is why we are more susceptible to infections/disease. Cortisol is a stress hormone in our body that helps our body respond to stress. When we are over stressed it weakens our immune system and our body can't fight as hard. Stress lowers the number of lymphocytes.There are two types of lymphocytes:

B cells- produce antibodies which are released into the fluid surrounding the body's cells to destroy the invading viruses and bacteria.

T cells- if the invader gets inside a cell, these (T cells) lock on to the infected cell, multiply and destroy it.

The immune system is a collection of billions of cells that travel through the bloodstream. They move in and out of tissues and organs defending the body against foreign bodies (antigens), such as bacteria, viruses and cancerous cells. If your health is important to you- as I'm sure it is, please stop worrying about your past and focus on the present and future. Pray more, worry less, take action.

It bothered me that I had not accomplished much, or lived up to certain standards: Graduate high school by age 18, finish college by age 24 depending on your degree level of choice, travel in your 30's, get married, and have kids. Preferably two kids, one boy, one girl. Buy a house in your 40's and prepare for retirement. Travel as a family so the kids can get the experience. Well I did not have any of these things by age forty, but the two kids and they were both boys. I am so glad that I have **forgiven myself** and am aware that it is never too late to live your dreams and have the desires of your heart.

It is not society who makes the rules of how our lives should be by a certain age. It is the desires of our hearts, our own wants and needs, and Gods will that determines the outcome of our lives. Do not live a fairy tale lifestyle or deadlines, make goals and accomplish them!!!

Holding on to my past caused anxiety and depression. I would have random panic attacks. Panic attacks can be one of the scariest experiences to go through. The attacks can range from a sudden surge of fear that only lasts a few minutes to heart palpitations and shortness of breath that mimic a heart attack. Untreated anxiety disorders can lead to extremely negative consequences that can impact a person's entire daily life. They may not be able to work, go to school, or have normal social relationships. People who have panic disorder may feel as though they are suffocating, having a heart attack, or going crazy. This was a horrible feeling. I am so grateful that I overcame it without medication.

Thinking of all the bad choices I had made, I would cry in the shower allowing my tears to drain with the water, then I get out the shower with a smile on my face so that my kids would not know I had been crying. I was so busy worried about things that I could not change, I forgot to focus on what I could do different so that I would not have to be in that same situation ever again. I forgot that I still had a present and a future. I allowed my past to consume me. I had become a pessimist, living in darkness, & hopeless. One day I looked in the mirror and said to myself, "I love you, I forgive you, and it is never too late to do better." As long as I was focused on all the mistakes I had made, time I had wasted on jobs that were not fulfilling and did not pay well, relationships that was supposed to be for a season, my age and what I had not yet accomplished, I could not move forward.

Nothing is ever as bad as it seems. How we handle things makes a big difference, and will determine how it affects us. Time truly does heal all wounds if we allow it to. Let go of regrets and say goodbye to the past forever!!!

Ladies we cannot change the past no matter how much we think about it, dwell in it, or think of how we could have been better off had we not made certain mistakes/decisions, or if things that were in and out of our control hadn't happened to us. We cannot enjoy the present, or look forward to the future, if we are living in the past. This is why the serenity prayer is so important, repeat after me:

God grant me the serenity to accept the things I cannot change; courage to change the things I can, and have the wisdom to know the difference, living one day at a time; enjoying one moment at a time.

JOURNEY 14

It was All for a Reason

I have learned over time with maturity and spiritual growth that all things happen for a reason. Everything that I encountered in my life, chose to do, mistakes I made, has built my character, strengthened me, and taught me lessons that will get me exactly to where I need to be.

In the words of John Mayer;

Someday everything will make perfect sense, so for now, laugh at the confusion, smile through your tears, be strong, and keep reminding yourself that everything happens for a reason!!!

I have learned that the more we try to lean on our own understanding instead of accepting life for what it is only makes it more difficult. So keep it simple.

JOURNEY 15

New Beginnings

❧

I have learned that I am not starting from scratch, I am starting from experience. This is my new beginning. I know better, so I am doing better. I cannot beat myself up about what I did not know, or mistakes that I cannot change, and neither should you. Learn from past mistakes, don't allow them to hinder you. **Regrets** will no longer be allowed to hinder me from my future. I will no longer risk taking my dreams to the grave with me, but instead, allow them to manifest. I will not be afraid to fail; hence I will not succeed. Failures are only teachings of what not to do again, how to do it different, or better.

I am over-joyed about my **new beginnings!!!**

I have completed book #1 which you are reading now and I am working on book numbers 2 & 3.

I am working on my campaign titled, **"Don't Cop Out!"** The fight against mass incarceration of minorities and the injustice that we face every day. These same injustices that some of my family and friends have faced. People cop out in exchange for freedom or to receive less time in jail, out of fear of losing their case, because justice is not always in our favor due to financial reasons as well as race. They say justice is blind, but I believe it sees very well.

I am the Sole Proprietor of More Than a Mentor, which will provide affordable holistic life coaching services to the people in my community and surrounding areas. I am observant, I listen to the cries of my community. My company represents hope, endurance, & change. I saw a need and I filled it. I am more than a life coach, I am more than a mentor, these are titles, I was blessed with the type of love that helps & heals. These are the services I provide:

- Guidance.
- Capitalize on your strengths.
- Overcome weaknesses.
- Establish & maintain healthy family relationships.

- Improve your thinking.

- Eliminate limiting beliefs.

- Clarify your goals and priorities.

- Develop empowering habits.

- Help to heal from past hurts, regrets, & disappointments.

- Working on the person piece by piece like a puzzle and just like a puzzle, the beauty of completion is an amazing masterpiece.

I am on fire and will not stop until I leave a blaze of change behind. I believe that this is the purpose that drives my life. It is fulfilling like nothing else I've ever done.

No more regrets ladies!!! We are moving forward with confidence and on a journey of New Beginnings!!

"The question isn't who is going to let me, it's who is going to stop me!" By Ayn Rand

Reflection:

_____

_____

_____

_____

_____

_____

_____

_____

_____

_____

_____

_____

_____

_____

_____

_____

_____

JOURNEY 16

Turning Passions into Hustles

❧

Proverbs 30:8 give me neither poverty nor riches! Give me just enough to satisfy my needs.

1. Taco Bell-cashier/team lead

2. 7-Eleven-cashier

3. Best Buy-lead cashier

4. First Bank of Oak Park-teller

5. Chicago Tribune-phone sales rep.

6. Marketing Solutions-survey rep.

7. Ticket Master-ticket sales phone rep

8. United Center-food prep/cashier

9. Cedar Point Nursing Home-dietary

10. Dunbar Armor-change order filler

11. Walgreens-head of cosmetics/cashier

12. Bank One, now Chase-operations clerk

13. TCF Bank-teller

14. Marshalls Department Store-lead cashier/C.S.R

15. Kelly Service-temp agency

16. Randstad-temp agency

17. Robert Half-temp agency

18. SNI Companies-temp agency

19. Salvation Army-teacher's assistant children ages 3-6

20. International Bank of Chicago-teller/operations analyst

21. LaSalle Network-temp agency

22. Started turning passions into hustles

I am sure lots of us can relate to this, especially the millennial generation. People job hop because they can't find their place in the workplace due to it always feels like something is missing and it is because most of us are not doing what we are passionate about.

I started working at age 17 thanks to a friend **Theresa Henry** who later became the mother to my oldest brothers' child. She gave me my first job at Taco Bell. Working at Taco Bell was the best work experience of my many jobs where the staff grew to be like a big happy family. We all supported one another emotionally and financially when needed. We built professional relationships that lasted into this current day and age. Two decades later we are still very close friends:

Marika, Wesley, Adolph, Falana, Ina, Doris, Felicia H., & Evelyn.

If you are wondering about that long list of companies at the start of this chapter, those are all the jobs I worked from age 17-47. I have beat myself up about being a job hopper when my reality is, I have a burning desire to do what I'm passionate about and working for companies that focuses on supply & demand, where the purpose is about making the company rich, is not important to me at all. My passion is to be a part of life changing events. To do God's will so that he gets the glory!

I am unveiling my talents and turning passions into hustles. We all have God given talents, we just have to ask that they be revealed to us.

When I started working in 1987, the minimum wage was $3.35 an hour. Although things were not as costly then as they are now, imagine trying to live on, and take care of a family from an hourly wage such as this. After thirty years of working, minimum wages have only gone up about $5 more since then. That's horrible in my opinion.

Wanting better wages could also help you in deciding to attend college, to earn a degree in a field that you are passionate about, so that you love what you do, and make good money while doing it. When you love what you do, it does not feel like work. You are not watching the clock all day counting down the time until you go home. College is best if you can earn your degree or degrees without ending up in lots of student loan debt. There are so many options these days to help with not settling for what is being offered, which is clearly not always enough to live on. Entrepreneurship is always an option as well, but not for everyone.

Let's look at the list below, which should help inspire you to use jobs as stepping stones to make money work for you, instead of working for money:

Paycor has created a breakdown by state.

State:

2019 Minimum Wage

2020 Minimum Wage

Alabama

$7.25 (Federal, no state minimum)

$7.25 (Federal, no state minimum)

Alaska

$9.89

$10.19

Arizona

$11.00

$12.00

Arkansas

$9.25

$10.00

California

$12.00*

$13.00*

Colorado

$11.10

$12.00

Connecticut

$11.00

$11.00 ($12.00 effective 9/1/20)

Delaware

$9.25

$9.25

Washington D.C.

$14.00

$14.00 ($15.00 effective 7/1/20)

Florida

$8.46

$8.56

Georgia

$5.15 (Employers subject to Fair Labor Standards Act must pay the $7.25 Federal minimum wage.)

$5.15 (Employers subject to the Fair Labor Standards Act must pay the $7.25 Federal minimum wage)

Hawaii

$10.10

$10.10

Idaho

$7.25

$7.25

Illinois

$8.25

$9.25

(**Chicago's** $13 per hour **minimum wage** to $14 per hour in July **2020** and to $15 in July 2021.)

Indiana

$7.25

$7.25

Iowa

$7.25

$7.25

Kansas

$7.25

$7.25

Kentucky

$7.25

$7.25

Louisiana

$7.25 (Federal, no state minimum)

$7.25 (Federal, no state minimum)

Maine

$11.00

$12.00

Maryland

$10.10

$11.00

Massachusetts

$12.00

$12.75

Michigan

$9.45

$9.65

Minnesota

$9.86**

$10.00**

Mississippi

$7.25 (Federal, no state minimum)

$7.25 (Federal, no state minimum)

Missouri

$8.60

$9.45

Montana

$8.50

$8.65

Nebraska

$9.00

$9.00

Nevada

$7.25***

$7.25***

New Hampshire

$7.25 (Federal, no state minimum)

$7.25 (Federal, no state minimum)

New Jersey

$10.00

$11.00

New Mexico

$7.50

$9.00

New York

$11.10

$11.80**** (statewide)

North Carolina

$7.25

$7.25

North Dakota

$7.25

$7.25

Ohio

$8.55

$8.70

Oklahoma

$7.25

$7.25

Oregon

$11.25****

$11.25****

Pennsylvania

$7.25

$7.25

Rhode Island

$10.50

$10.50

South Carolina

$7.25 (Federal, no state minimum)

$7.25 (Federal, no state minimum)

South Dakota

$9.10

$9.30

Tennessee

$7.25 (Federal, no state minimum)

$7.25 (Federal, no state minimum)

Texas

$7.25

$7.25

Utah

$7.25

$7.25

Vermont

$10.78

$10.96

Virginia

$7.25

$7.25

Washington

$12.00

$13.50

West Virginia

$8.75

$8.75

Wisconsin

$7.25

$7.25

Wyoming

$5.15 (Employers subject to Fair Labor Standards Act must pay the Federal minimum wage.)

$5.15 (Employers subject to the Fair Labor Standards Act must pay the $7.25 Federal minimum wage)

$13.00 rate is for California employers with 26 or more employees. Employers in California with 25 or less employees have a minimum wage of $12.00 per hour.

$10.00 rate is for large employers. Small employers have a minimum wage of $8.15 per hour.

$7.25 rate is for Nevada employees who are offered health insurance. $8.25 rate is for Nevada employees who are not offered health insurance. On July 1, 2020, the minimum wage for employees with health insurance will increase to $8.00. The minimum wage for employees without health insurance will increase to $9.00.

****Statewide minimum wages apply in areas that are not governed by a higher, local minimum wage ordinance. New York City and Portland Metro are examples of areas which have local minimum wage rates that exceed the statewide minimum****

This is to show what we are expected to survive on. With time being so valuable & precious, to trade it for money doesn't balance out in my opinion. Do what you love so it won't seem like work, it will feel as if you are getting paid to do what you love. Unless we take the road less traveled, tap into our talents, and make our money work for us, we will be caught in the rat race. I was brainwashed into believing that living check to check was normal, that working to pay rent and bills until we die was systematic. It didn't seem like an American dream to me. The fear of thinking that this was considered living, made me change my mindset when it came to money. I want to live a life of abundance and there was nothing abundant about this.

Not having the knowledge and tools to know what to do with money is our greatest downfall. If I had someone to teach me and had been mature enough to listen and apply it to my everyday life, there is no way I would have been in the predicament that I was in recently. I have taught myself how to make money work for me. It is a work in progress for late bloomers/learners, but it is never too late.

Embarrassed to say, but proud to admit, I have had over a $110K from age 33-43. Work wages are **not** included in this total. This amount is from blessings from God in my opinion. This money included back pay, law suits, class action suits, and lottery winnings. Imagine if I had financially literacy with this type of money within a 10 year span. Yeah, I can imagine what you're thinking, I beat myself up about it for years, but that's in the past. I learned from my mistakes and I have moved forward. Don't get me wrong, I did lots of good with the money.

- I helped my family
- Friends
- Charities
- Church/pastor
- Started my own mentoring program which I self-funded
- Traveled
- Cars that I could have paid for in full, but chose not to
- Paid rent & bills up 6 months

My biggest mistake/downfall was that I didn't have the knowledge to invest, or make my money grow as I do now. My goal is to teach my children and anyone willing to listen and learn so that you all won't make the same mistakes as I have. Are you all tired yet???

When I think about the way things are set up as far as the pay scale made up by America, the cost of living made up by those same people, it just doesn't balance out. The design is for the rich to stay rich and the poor to stay poor, but with the right tools and mindset we have the power to live however we choose, but if we pretend like the deck is not stacked against us, then maybe we're just stuck in the American dream that seems to have become a nightmare for most.

Why is it a dream that comes true for some, but a nightmare for others? This is my empirical evidence (based on observation, and experience, rather than theory, and logic):

Dream:

- People who were taught about finance, credit, stock, investments, and how to make money work for them.
- People with drive & ambition.
- People who don't settle.
- Optimist.
- Born into rich family/or marry rich.
- Takes the road less traveled.
- Parent who knew the importance of building generational wealth for their children.

Nightmare:

- Depends solely on what was taught to them, instead of seeking knowledge.

- Hopeless, unmotivated.

- Settle for whatever they can get, feels undeserving.

- Pessimist.

- Born into a poor family.

- Never step outside the box, doesn't venture out.

- Doesn't save money at all.

I can go on and on, but these are examples of the two types of dreamers. I have also learned that you have to pay yourself first no matter what your pay rate is. We travel in rain, sleet, snow, or extreme weather to make money. Some of us have young children, depending on our schedule, we don't see them until late in the evening. Work can put wear & tear on your body depending on the type of work you do. Working on computers can put wear and tear on your eyes, hands, wrist, fingers, and even your back, depending on the type of chair your employer provides. None of us knows what the future holds, so we can't depend on social security, disability, pension, 401k, or any government funds. All these funds have risk. With the debt that our country is allegedly in according to the US deficit. We can only depend on ourselves.

My advice is:

To not live above your means, save money, learn to invest, learn to make money work for you verses having the mindset to work for money, don't spend so much money on material things, and know the importance of things that appreciate & depreciate with time.

I no longer have limits or fears. I had a sit-down talk with fear and demanded it give me back all my hopes & dreams. Because of the power in my voice it released everything I allowed it to take from me. Fear is no longer welcome in my life!!!

Some people will take all the odds and turn them in their favor. They will take the negatives in life and turn them into positives. They will teach themselves everything that nobody taught them. They will learn from what they saw negative and go in the opposite direction. Unfortunately, everybody is not equipped mentally or determined enough to do the opposite of what was around them their entire young lives.

Here are the steps to success:

- Believe in yourself.

- Accept failure as a part of success

- Demonstrate two qualities: Discipline & Determination/Undefeatable determination!

- Recognize your gifts.

- Set goals and complete them. Vision boards are good to prepare so that you have a visual reminder.

- Dedicate yourself to the process no matter how long it takes.

- Trust God to bless your efforts.

Change Your Mindset:

Having the mindset to work just to pay bills & rent should be stone-age thinking. Please do away with that type of thinking. To do what you love and be paid well for it is the new way of thinking/living. Nobody I know has become financially free or rich from working a job. Not saying that it is not possible, but I have not seen or heard of it.

I want to see people doing what they love and enjoying life in full capacity. Struggle should not be consistent.

I am turning passions into hustles with writing books to uplift and give advice to girls & women. I am starting a profitable business that will allow consumers to purchase my books & t-shirts with my inspirational & entrepreneur quotes. I am an affordable holistic life coach. I now own over a 100 shares of stock and learning to invest and make money work for me.

I am proud of me!!! As you work on yourself and accomplish goals, whether big or small, celebrate them all, because you deserve it. I want the best for all people who strive to do better and want life in abundance, so I will mentor to the world as long as I am able. I love people with a special kind of love that is hard to explain, but shown through my actions as a humanitarian. I care about the well-being of others.

MOVE FORWARD TURNING YOUR PASSIONS INTO HUSTLES!!!

Reflection:

_____

_____

_____

_____

_____

_____

_____

_____

_____

_____

_____

_____

_____

_____

_____

_____

_____

_____

_____

Employee:

Leave Benefits

Leave benefits are the times available each year for the employee to have some time out and enjoy paid time when they are not working for their employer. They may take a vacation or choose to work on their personal relationships, hobbies, or simply rest. Vacations can give employees the chance to really take stock of their lives and refresh themselves. This means that when they return to work, they will have more focus and energy to complete their daily tasks with a new vigor and satisfaction.

*My issue with this: There is 365/366 days in a year and most jobs allow 5-20 days of vacation depending on your time with the company. Rarely 20, but I have heard of it. Depending on the amount of stress from work and everyday living vacation is needed more often than what employers provide. Not only that, to travel often should be on everybody's bucket list, near or far, travel is a much needed experience in my opinion.

Guaranteed Income

A huge advantage of employment vs entrepreneurship is guaranteed income. This fixed amount of money deposited on a weekly, bi-weekly, or monthly basis into bank accounts means financial security for the employee and their family. Employers pay the employee for their services towards their organization. This pay often includes a range of allowances and benefits which may include, taxes, insurance, health insurance, provident funds and company shares. Sometimes the family of the employee will also be covered by a health plan. Even after the age of retirement, the employee may continue to get private or state income, leaving them and their families secure for the rest of their lives.

*My issue with this: Nothing is guaranteed! Illinois has a fire at will policy, which means for no reason at all. Downsizing or cutting back is usually the reason for layoffs. Most times, depending on the company, they will deny or fight your unemployment benefits as if you don't have rent, bills, etc. to pay. Having no income will surely affect your livelihood. I know this first hand because I suffered 4 months with $0 income.

Fixed Working Hours

Employees will often agree on fixed working hours that will be guaranteed and outlined in a contract between themselves and the organization that employs them. Overtime or extra hours will be worked at the employee's discretion and will not be compulsory. Hours exceeding that in the contract are called 'overtime' and are often remunerated at a rate higher than the standard hours agreed when employment begins. Sometimes an agreement is set out between an employer and employee to receive time in exchange for working hours that exceed that of their contract. Hours worked can be saved and exchanged for longer periods of holiday or extra days off work.

*My issue with this: Saying it would not be compulsory, which means; the law or mandatory, but this is not true for all companies, because I'm sure most of us has heard of mandatory overtime. Also, depending on the company you work for, business hours are usually during the time that you need to take care of your own business, like 9-5pm or 8-6pm. When do we get to take care of our own business, or are we forced to work at night? Mothers with kids usually face things like; doctor visit for a check- up/illness, personal business, appointments for your child (Ren), report card pickup, sporting event for your child, etc. Not only have that, when the allotted time given to you runs out, the days you miss counted against you, which could lead to termination.

Bereavement time is usually 3 days, although some employers are more generous and sympathetic to your loss, I think three days is heartless. I know people who lost their dog/cat and needed more time off than that. (Seriously, people love their pets) God forbid, but unfortunately, it can be family, and you expect me to heal, or be back to normal after three days. For some people this is realistic, they take death for what is, it happens, but not all have that strength, or mindset to function this way. When my father passed in December of 2008, it rocked my world. I wasn't coping well with his death for about 3 weeks. I couldn't return to work with the state of mind I was in, so I was terminated!

Less Responsibility

In employment, you are often assigned a particular role and are only responsible for performing the tasks that are directly related to that role whilst you are working. You don't need to interfere or worry with how other people are performing across the company, as you will still receive your payment as long as you complete all the tasks that are expected and outlined for your individual role. You will probably be periodically appraised for your role and this will affect your chances of promotion and also your success rate within your profession. Appraisals can be a good opportunity to discover your individual strengths and weaknesses.

*My issue with this: Now-a-days we wear many hats on the job. Not like the good ole days, when you had a title, and did only that one or two duties. These days you are doing way more work, but pay is the same. So, claiming that working for an employer is less responsibility, is an over statement. If you're an entrepreneur at least you're building your own empire/company and setting goals to make yourself rich, versus a company that will never be yours. I have never heard of someone becoming rich being an employee, even with advancements/appraisals.

Entrepreneur:

Growth in Career

As an entrepreneur, you have the ability to fulfill your goals and aspirations as an individual. You will not have a boss in place to interfere or make decisions for you. Your life is your own and the amount and size of the risks that you take is your choice.

Entrepreneurs all have the opportunity to rule their chosen business sector. Obviously, this is decided by the market demand for their product or service along with the amount of drive and determination harbored by the individual.

Independent

With no boss in place, the entrepreneur is free to make their own decisions in both their personal and professional life. They can work whenever they want, however many hours they want, and sometimes from wherever they want.

They will be able to direct employees and have other people helping them to make money and achieve their goals.

However, they will need to be natural leaders and set up standards along with roles and responsibilities for their employees. The more they can outsource, the easier their life will become.

Flexible Working Hours

Ultimately, the entrepreneur will choose working hours that suit them. While some entrepreneurs will work 80-hour weeks when they first start out, others will have the people and resources in place to sit back and work as little as possible.

The Ability to Earn

The financial growth for an entrepreneur is much greater than that of an employee constrained to a salary or an hourly rate decided and agreed on at the start of their employment.

They will own their company outright and often have a large share of the business profits.

They have the potential to earn as much as they want to, depending on the demand for their product or services.

Change and Exploration

If an entrepreneur sees a new opportunity to make more money by expanding or re-training, they have the choice to do so.

Entrepreneurs are often out networking and making new business contacts and opportunities. This means they are the creators of their own destiny and can always change and explore new horizons.

I admit that entrepreneurship is not for everyone. There is lots of risk, as well as rewards. This is a clear example of taking the road less traveled. I know people who work part time in their career field, but is an entrepreneur fulltime because they found their passion after choosing a career. My advice is to follow your dreams whatever they are.

Whatever road you choose to take in life to make money, make sure it is what you love, your talent, and your passion. If we just work for money it will not make us happy, whether it is for a company or for yourself. I cannot reiterate enough, DO WHAT YOU LOVE!!!

**THE END, OR SHOULD I SAY,
"HAPPY NEW BEGINNINGS!"**

Reference Page:

www.paycor.com

www.google.com

www.psycologytoday.com

www.medium.com

psycnet.apa.org

www.ingramcontent.com/pod-product-compliance
Lightning Source LLC
Chambersburg PA
CBHW050729030426
42336CB00012B/1474